About This Book

Title: *Kinds of Sounds*

Step: 6

Word Count: 213

Skills in Focus: /ow/ and /oi/ diphthongs

Tricky Words: ball, falls, into, animals, talk, some

Ideas For Using This Book

Before Reading:
- **Comprehension:** Look at the title and cover image together. Walk through the pictures in the book with readers and have them make predictions about what they might learn while reading.
- **Accuracy:** Practice reading the tricky words listed on page 1.
- **Phonics:** Tell students they will read words with /ow/ and /oi/ diphthongs. Explain that a diphthong is two vowel sounds that are squished together. The letter combinations *oy* and *oi* make the same diphthong sound. The letters *ow* and *ou* make another diphthong sound. Write these letter combinations on a piece of paper. Then write the story words *oink, sound, coin, loud, boy, bounces, voice, toy, chow, cow,* and *down*. Have readers point to the letter combinations making the diphthong in each word. Then have readers look through the first few pages to see if they can find any other examples of words with /ow/ and /oi/ diphthongs.

During Reading:
- Have readers point under each word as they read it.
- **Decoding:** If readers are stuck on a word, help them say each sound and blend the sounds together smoothly. Be sure to point out words with /ow/ and /oi/ diphthongs as they appear. On page 21, readers may need support with the phrase "slows down." The letter combination *ow* makes a different sound in each word.
- **Comprehension:** Invite readers to talk about new things they are learning about sounds while reading. What are they learning that they didn't know before?

After Reading:
Discuss the book. Some ideas for questions:
- What different kinds of sounds have you heard before? What are some places where you might hear these sounds?
- What do you still wonder about sounds?

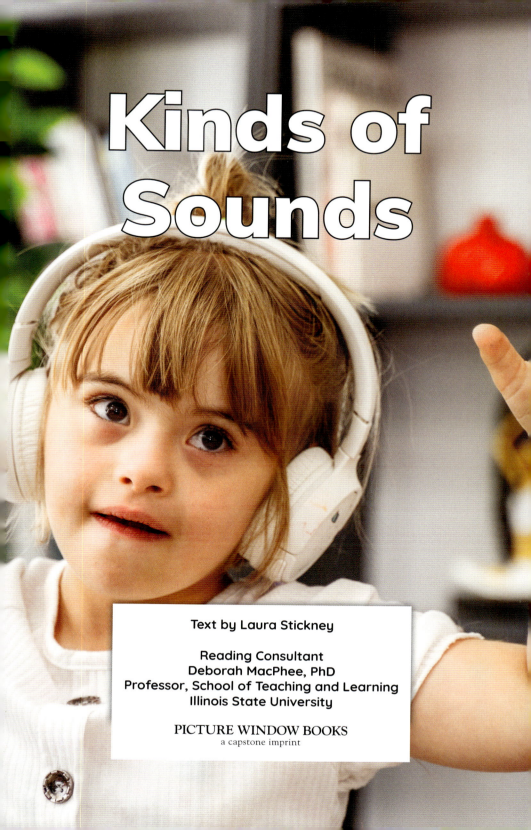

Kinds of Sounds

Text by Laura Stickney

Reading Consultant
Deborah MacPhee, PhD
Professor, School of Teaching and Learning
Illinois State University

PICTURE WINDOW BOOKS
a capstone imprint

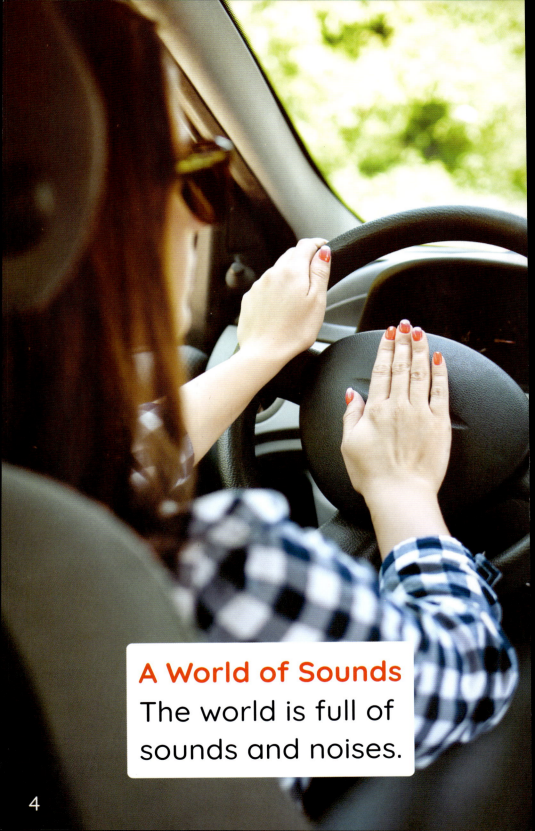

A World of Sounds
The world is full of sounds and noises.

Cars honk. Dogs bark and howl. Toilets flush.

When a ball bounces, it makes a noise. Boing!

When a boy flips a coin, it falls down and makes a noise. Clink!

When a clown hits a drum, it makes a noisy crash. Bang!

When a cat eats food out of its dish, you can hear it chow and meow.

How Do We Hear Noises?

People can hear noises with their ears.

Sounds travel in waves. The sound waves bounce off things.

Then the sound waves go into your ears. The noises hit your eardrum.

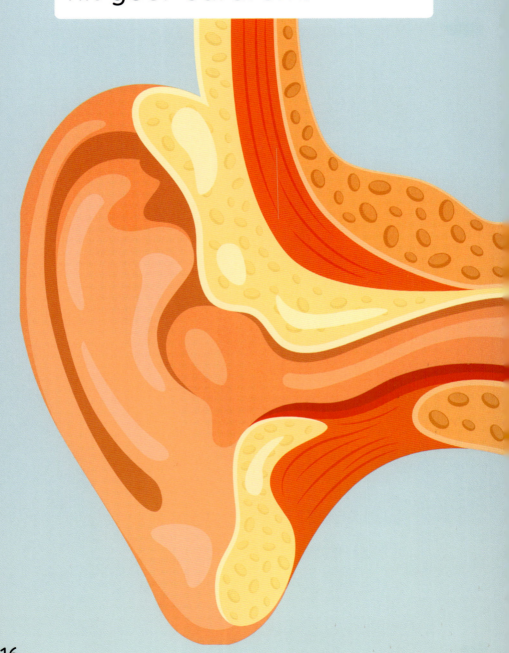

Your brain tells you what the noises are.

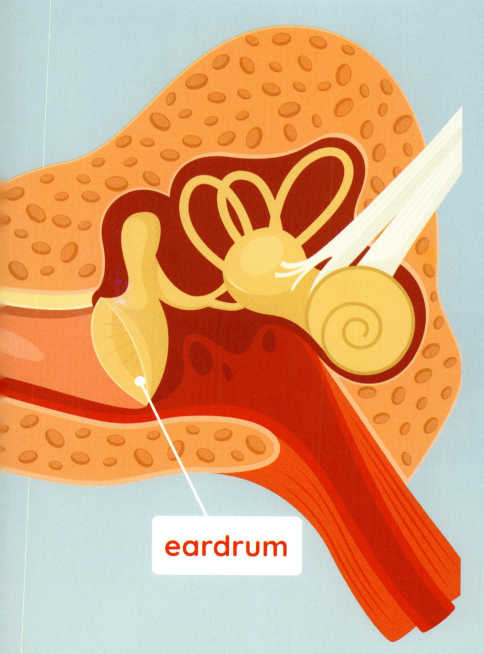

eardrum

Making Sounds

Sounds can be loud.

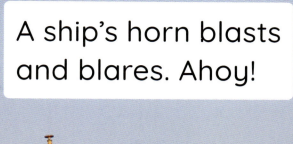

A ship's horn blasts and blares. Ahoy!

A train makes a noisy screech when it slows down.

Sounds can be soft too. Your voice can whisper.

Rain patters down on the roof.

Animals make lots of noises. They make noises to talk with each other.

Some animals make noises when they hunt.

Owls hoot and coo.
Pigs oink.

Brown bears growl.
Cows moo.

People can make lots of sounds with their voices.

Wow! Noises are neat. How many sounds can you make with your voice?

More Ideas:

Phonics Activity

Writing with /ow/ and /oi/ Diphthongs:
Ask readers to write a story using as many words as possible that have /ow/ and /oi/ diphthongs. The story can be as silly or serious as readers want!

Suggested words:

/ow/: howl, down, chow, how, owl, brown, cow, wow, growl

/oi/: noise, toilet, coin, voice, oink, boy, joy, toy, enjoy

Extended Learning Activity

Studying Sounds:
Have readers go outside and notice the different sounds they hear. Ask them to write down the sounds they hear on a piece of paper. Then have them write a few sentences about what each sound is like. Is it loud or soft? Challenge readers to use words with /ow/ and /oi/ diphthongs in their sentences.

Published by Picture Window Books, an imprint of Capstone
1710 Roe Crest Drive, North Mankato, Minnesota 56003
capstonepub.com

Copyright © 2026 by Capstone.
All rights reserved. No part of this publication may be reproduced in whole or in part, or stored in a retrieval system, or transmitted in any form or by any means, electronic, mechanical, photocopying, recording, or otherwise, without written permission of the publisher.

Library of Congress Cataloging-in-Publication Data is available on the Library of Congress website.

ISBN: 9798875227233 (hardback)
ISBN: 9798875231209 (paperback)
ISBN: 9798875231186 (eBook PDF)

Image Credits: Getty: Jose Luis Pelaez/Stone, cover; iStock: BackyardProduction, 8–9, Chong Kee Siong, 28, DIGIcal, 30, HuntImages, 24, John Rowley, 29, JohnPitcher, 27, kali9, 22, 32, karen crewe, 25, Lubo Ivanko, 20–21, Phynart Studio, 2–3, SDI Productions, 6–7, Zinkevych, 1, 14; Shutterstock: alirizaozcelik, 19, ANURAK PONGPATIMET, 12–13, everydayplus, 18, Fabio Principe, 15, Ivan Larshin, 5, Mikkel Holck, 26, nikolaborovic, 4, Numpon Jumroonsiri, 23, Sharif Pavlov, 10–11, Twinkle picture, 16–17

Printed and bound in China. 6274